MW00427490

THE CRICKET FLOURS COOKBOOK

"All Cricket, No BULL..."

Second Edition

By Charles B. Wilson

ISBN-13: 978-1533386816

ISBN-10: 1533386811

CONTENTS

Foreword

To make a long story short (and explain how I got here), I love my daughter. People have their better halves. She has my essence, but with an extra strong dose of fearlessness. I would like to say I would do anything for her. But if it's ridiculous, she knows my "Forget it" look. But I will never forget, we were bundled up and on our way home from dinner at our favorite restaurant in her neck of the woods in New York City, when she said "Mom! You need to talk to KT's brother – he's got this great food startup." Needless to say, as you now know, I gave her a "well okay then" look. I'm glad I did.

So, I connected with Cricket Flours LLC founder, Charles Wilson, through my daughter, Merrin. As a chef of more than 30 years with an emphasis on cooking without fear or intimation, these guys knew I wouldn't turn up my nose at the concept of cooking with milled insects. But, crickets? Crickets.

All chefs love to experiment, take risks - it's what makes us who we are. I'm all about bold when it comes to food research, but I was quick to discover this trend is more reasonable than it is bold. It's innovative, but completely rational. Like they say, "No Bull". The culinary community and everyday cooking enthusiasts (or survivalists) will appreciate how Cricket Flours LLC has conceptualized a line of quality products; with a collection of recipes I wholeheartedly endorse. And, yes, the products are packed with protein and have an impressive nutritional resume. I will be encouraging my own students at my cooking studio to trust me on this one. I've made a career of cooking without a parachute with stupid easy and delicious recipes. This cook book juxtaposes my no stress style with a sophisticated and powerful play on some damn fine dishes and a new appreciation for crickets!

Candace Conley

www.TheGirlCanCookSchool.com

Introduction

Welcome to the second edition of The Cricket Flour Cookbook, *"All Cricket, No BULL…"* from CricketFlours.com. This book is our second release and is inspired by our desire to bring some of our favorite family recipes to your kitchen using a sustainable and environmentally-friendly source of protein and nutrition: Cricket Protein.

Since launching our business and website at www.CricketFlours.com, we have received thousands of questions, emails, likes, shares, etc. regarding our full line of products. Because we use such a new ingredient in our western culture, we have a lot of people wondering what exactly are we doing? What do our products taste like? How do you bake with crickets? Because we use crickets, not a lot of people have had an opportunity to try it before or in our products such as our Cricket Flours: 100% Pure, Cricket Instant Oatmeal, Cricket Brownie Mix, etc. We have had people from over 180+ countries come visit our website to check out our new recipes, videos, products and content. While 80% of the world currently incorporates insects into their diets, this is still a new and emerging trend in the United States. People in the U.S. are searching for alternative sources of protein and nutrition, but there is still a hurdle facing companies that use insects: *"The Ick Factor."*

If you look at the small handful of insect-based protein bars or desserts, you are unlikely to find one that is "insect flavored." Although cricket flour and cricket powder has a neutral or slightly nutty taste, these products use tantalizing flavors such as Blueberry, Strawberry, Vanilla, Chocolate, or Cinnamon… i.e. flavors that your taste buds can identify with.

That is the goal of our cricket protein recipe book. We aim to deliver delicious recipes that inspire your taste buds and motivate you to try incorporating cricket powder into some of your favorite meals. While we are creating more recipes each week, we want to share some of our newest recipes with our customers and readers. With recipes such as our Bacon Infused Cheese Muffins, Chocolate Espresso Banana Bread, Antioxidant Smoothie, Balsamic Fig Dressing, Spicy Baked Peppers, and Hazelnut Liquor Cake, we know you are going to love trying some of these amazing creations.

WHAT THIS BOOK IS NOT

This cookbook is not written for people who are culinary experts or renowned chefs. You will not find complicated cooking directions or see obscure ingredients being used for novelty's sake in these dishes. Instead, each recipe is straightforward and written so that you can easily create these delicious dishes to try and share with your family and friends.

WHAT IS UNIQUE ABOUT THIS BOOK?

Most cookbooks are designed using sumptuous pictures and descriptions that help inspire readers to explore new ways of cooking. We are doing exactly the same, but we're using cricket powder to add new tastes, textures, protein and nutrition to each of our recipes. To create this cookbook, I have spent hundreds of hours in the kitchen experimenting and refining each and every recipe you see. The goal is to demystify this protein superfood so that you can begin using it in new ways that your family will love.

I am excited for you to try out each of these recipes and look forward to hearing what you think. Enjoy!

-Best,

Charles B. Wilson
Founder & CEO

P.S. Feel free to reach out to me to ask questions about the cookbook's content or what we are doing at Charles@CricketFlours.com and I will get back to you personally.

Welcome

"For some businesses, the sound of crickets means it's the end…for us, it means we are just getting started!"

- Charles B. Wilson

Cooking with Cricket Powder

Welcome! We are excited to share some of our favorite cricket powder recipes with you from our new cookbook titled, "All Cricket, No BULL…" This cookbook is separated into six different parts to provide a general framework for the recipes.

WHAT IS CRICKET FLOUR?

Before anyone starts cooking and baking with cricket powder, it is important to know what it is. Cricket flour or cricket powder, is made from finely milled crickets raised for human consumption. The name can be misleading — it is important to remember that cricket flour cannot be used as a one-for-one substitute for normal wheat or baking flours. When shopping for cricket powder to use in your own baking recipes and creations, you may find that it is also called cricket protein, cricket flour, or cricket protein powder.

HOW DOES CRICKET POWDER AFFECT RECIPES?

Cooking and baking with cricket powder is a great way to incorporate more protein and nutrition into your favorite meals and recipes. However, like any ingredient, adding cricket flour to your recipes will give it different attributes. In a broad sense, when cricket powder is used in baking, it functions similarly to coconut flour or baking powder.

Similarly to using coconut flour, you will want to make sure that you do not substitute 100% of cricket powder for your normal baking flour. In general, you will want to make sure that your normal baking flour mix, wheat or gluten-free, accounts for at least 70% of the mix when using cricket flour. Too much cricket protein will affect the density and the liquid requirements for your recipes. While this may be the goal of a new recipe you are working on, it is something to take into account when working cricket powder into existing recipes.

Additionally, cricket powder displays characteristics similar to baking powder. For most of our recipes, we have found that reducing the baking powder by half works well to get those same properties that you expect from a great muffin or bread recipe.

PART

One

Muffins, Loaves, and Morning Cakes

Muffins, Loaves, and Morning Cakes

Rise and shine! With so many cereals and baked goods on the market, it's easy to forget about including protein in your breakfast. The following cricket powder recipes give you the best of both worlds. Our muffins, loaves, and morning cakes are perfect for breakfast, brunch, or an afternoon snack. These recipes feature our customers' favorites, such as the Bacon Infused Cheese Muffins, Spiced French Toast, and instructions for blending and making your own fortified Cricket Flours: All-Purpose Baking Flour that you can use in any of your favorite baking recipes. Enjoy!

All-Purpose Baking Flour

Chocolate Espresso Banana Bread

Cinnamon Roll Sweet Bread

Cinnamon Cricket Flour Muffins

Chocolate Chip Pumpkin Muffins

Spiced French Toast

Cricket Flour Pancakes

Gluten Free Banana Pancakes with Cricket Protein

Spiced Granola with Cricket Flour

Bacon Infused Cheese Muffins

Blueberry Cricket Protein Muffins

Mini Lemon & Valencia Orange Raspberry Scones

"I tried the cricket protein powder the other day at a start up event. I was quite impressed by the taste. However, I am even more excited about the Eco-friendly alternative to existing protein powders.
Keep up the good work!"

- **Eric Harvey**

All-Purpose Baking Cricket Flour

Prep time: 5 minutes

All-Purpose Baking Flour

Amp up the nutrients in your favorite baked goods recipes with cricket protein. On our website and blog, we have received many questions about making a cricket powder that you can bake with. Because cricket powder is made from 100% crickets, you will need to mix it with other baking flours to get those same attributes you love in your cooking.

Use your favorite baking flour to mix with our Cricket Flours: 100% Pure in order to make your own All-Purpose Baking Flour. Using cricket protein you can generally replace 0-30% of your normal baking flour with our Cricket Flours: 100% Pure for added protein and nutrition to your favorite family recipes.

Ingredients:

- ∞ ²/₃ cup all-purpose flour
- ∞ ¹/₃ cup Cricket Flours: 100% Pure

Directions:

1. Mix ²/₃ cup all-purpose baking flour and ¹/₃ cup Cricket Flours: 100% Pure in a standard mixing bowl. It's that easy!
2. Use this ratio to make your own batches of all-purpose baking cricket flour to use in future recipes.

Chocolate Espresso Banana Bread

Prep time: 10 minutes
Cooking time: 50 minutes
Yield: 1 loaf

Chocolate Espresso Banana Bread

Ever worry about bruised bananas or letting them get overly ripe? Don't! They are perfect for banana bread, and this recipe delivers an enticing combination of flavors of banana, chocolate, and a hint of espresso.

Ingredients:

- 3-4 very ripe bananas
- 1 ½ all purpose baking flour
- ½ cup coconut sugar
- ½ cup brown sugar
- 1/3 cup melted butter
- 1 egg

- 3 tablespoons Cricket Flours: Peruvian Chocolate
- 1 shot of espresso
- 1 teaspoon vanilla extract
- 1 teaspoon baking soda
- 1 pinch sea salt

Directions:

1. Preheat oven to 350°F.
2. In a mixing bowl combine the bananas and melted butter until fully mixed.
3. Next add in and mix together the baking soda, salt, brown sugar, coconut sugar, and 1 egg well beaten.
4. Follow by adding in the vanilla extract, 1 shot of espresso cooled to room temperature, cricket powder, and baking flour to mix all together.
5. Lightly grease a 4in x 8in bread pan and add in the final mixture. Set on the middle over rack and bake for 50 minutes. Enjoy!

Cinnamon Roll Sweet Bread

Prep time: 3-4 hours
Cooking time: 35-40 minutes
Yield: 1 loaf

Cinnamon Roll Sweet Bread

As a family holiday favorite, this cinnamon roll sweet bread is a delicious treat. This bread recipe is filled with delicious cinnamony swirls that can be served with the main meals, as a dessert, or to make awe-inspiring French toast the next morning for the whole family.

Ingredients:

- ¼ cup warm water
- 1 package active dry yeast
- ¾ cup milk
- ½ cup sugar
- 8 tablespoons unsalted butter
- 1 teaspoon salt
- 1 egg
- 4 cups Cricket Flours: All Purpose Baking Flour
- 2 tablespoons cinnamon
- ½ cup brown sugar

Directions:

1. In a mixing bowl combine ¼ cup warm water and 1 packaged of active dry yeast and let sit for 5 minutes.
2. Stir in ¾ cup room temperature milk, ¼ cup sugar, 1 teaspoon salt, 4 tablespoons room temperature melted butter and 1 egg.
3. Next stir in 4 cups of Cricket Flours: All Purpose Baking Flour.
4. On a lightly floured bread board, turn out the dough and kneed gently. Place the kneaded dough in a lightly greased bowl, and turn over once. Cover the bowl with a kitchen cloth, and set near warm light to rise for 60-90 minutes until it has doubled in size.
5. Once doubled, punch down the dough and flip over to let it rise again for 60-90 minutes.
6. Remove the dough from the bowl and turn it out on the floured bread board, rolling it until the dough is about ½ inch in thickness. Spread 4 tablespoons of softened butter evenly across the dough, and evenly add the 2 tablespoons cinnamon, ¼ cup sugar, and ½ cup brown sugar.
7. Starting along the long edge of the dough, begin rolling the dough to create those cinnamony swirls. Pinch off the ends of the roll and fold 2 inches from each end under the bread loaf before placing it in a lightly greased bread pan. Cover the bread pan and let raise for a 3rd and final time until it has doubled to get the light and fluffy texture.
8. Preheat oven to 350°F.
9. Set on the middle over rack and bake for 35-40 minutes. Enjoy!

Cinnamon Cricket Flour Muffins

Prep time: 15 minutes
Cooking time: 21 minutes
Yield: 12 muffins

Cinnamon Cricket Flour Muffins

Which spice shouts "Breakfast!" more than cinnamon? Our Cinnamon Cricket Flour Muffins are packed with protein and nutrients. Apart from cricket flour, the cinnamon, milk, and eggs in these muffins contribute their fair share to the health factor. If you want yours to be extra indulgent, after they cool a bit, simply brush the top of each muffin with melted butter and dip into a cinnamon-sugar mixture. Enjoy!

Ingredients:

- 2 cups Cricket Flours: All Purpose Baking Flour
- ½ cup water
- ²/₃ cup milk
- ½ cup canola oil
- 1 tablespoon vanilla
- 2 eggs
- 1 teaspoon cinnamon
- 1 teaspoon salt
- 2 teaspoon baking soda
- 2 teaspoon baking powder
- ½ cup sugar

Directions:

1. Preheat oven to 350°F.
2. Line a standard muffin tin with paper muffin cups and grease paper cups with baking spray or butter.
3. In a standard mixing bowl, combine and fully mix all dry ingredients and make an indentation in the center.
4. Add water, milk, canola oil, vanilla and eggs to dry ingredients and gently mix until smooth.
5. Add ¹/₃ cup of batter to each muffin cup.
6. Place the muffin tin on the center rack of the oven for 20-22 minutes.
7. After 20-22 minutes, use a toothpick to make sure the muffins are finished cooking. The toothpick or fork should come out clean without any batter.
8. Remove muffins from the oven and let stand for 10-15 minutes before adding any toppings.

Chocolate Chip Pumpkin Muffins

Prep time: 10 minutes
Cooking time: 15-18 minutes
Yield: 12 muffins

Chocolate Chip Pumpkin Muffins

Inspired by the Official Pumpkin Day on October 26th, we decided to create a new pumpkin muffin recipe using some of our favorite ingredients but with an added twist! For this recipe we switched out the vegetable oil for applesauce, and the water for orange juice to give your muffins the right amount of moisture but with added flavors. Enjoy!

Ingredients:

- ¾ cup packed brown sugar
- 2 eggs
- ¼ cup orange juice
- ¾ teaspoon baking powder
- ½ teaspoon ground cloves
- ¼ teaspoon sea salt
- ½ cup semisweet chocolate chips
- ¼ cup unsweetened applesauce
- 1 cup canned organic pumpkin
- 1 ½ cups Cricket Flours: All Purpose Baking Flour
- ½ teaspoon baking soda
- 1 ¼ teaspoons ground cinnamon
- ½ teaspoon ground nutmeg

Directions:

1. Preheat oven to 400°F.
2. Mix together the brown sugar, oil, and eggs. Next add in the pumpkin and orange juice and mix until combined.
3. In a separate mixing bowl add the Cricket Flours: All Purpose Baking Flour and mix together the remaining dry ingredients.
4. Add the dry ingredients to the wet mixture and once mixed together, fold in the 1/2 cup chocolate chips.
5. Spoon the batter into slightly greased muffin tins about 2/3 to the top, and bake on the middle rack for 15-18 minutes.

Spiced French Toast

Prep time: 5 minutes
Cooking time: 2-4 minutes
Yield: 8

Spiced French Toast

Having company over for the weekend? Make this, and they'll be coming back for more—maybe more often than you like! Spiced French Toast is quick and tasty, showcasing a terrific blend of flavors. In each savory bite, you will taste the perfect combination of cinnamon, nutmeg, and vanilla on top of the eggy fried bread. This recipe is perfected when paired with maple syrup, fresh berries, and a side of sausage.

Ingredients:

- 8 slices of bread
- 2 eggs
- $^1/_3$ cup milk
- 1 teaspoon Cricket Flours: 100% Pure
- 1 teaspoon cinnamon
- ½ teaspoon vanilla extract
- 1 dash nutmeg

Directions:

1. In medium mixing bowl, combine eggs, milk, Cricket Flours: 100% Pure, cinnamon, vanilla, and nutmeg. Whisk all ingredients together until fully mixed.
2. Heat a lightly oiled pan over medium-high heat.
3. Taking a slice of bread, quickly dip each side in egg mixture and place in hot pan.
4. Cook each side for approximately 30-45 seconds, or until golden brown. Serve warm.

Cricket Flour Pancakes

Prep time: 5 minutes
Cooking time: 15 minutes
Yield: 6-8 pancakes

Cricket Flour Pancakes

Try out these Cricket Flour Pancakes and your go-to mix or recipe just won't cut it anymore. These pancakes take only 5 minutes to prepare and taste delicious with a hint of vanilla. Want pancakes on a weekday? Mix the batter the night before and refrigerate overnight. Fry them up in the morning, and you've got a well-fueled day ahead of you.

Ingredients:

- ∞ 1 ½ cups Cricket Flours: All Purpose Baking Flour
- ∞ 3 ½ teaspoons baking powder
- ∞ ¾ teaspoon salt
- ∞ 1 egg

- ∞ 3 tablespoon butter, melted
- ∞ 1 ¼ cups milk
- ∞ 1 teaspoon vanilla extract
- ∞ 1 ½ tablespoons sugar
- ∞

Directions:

1. Mix all dry ingredients in a large bowl.
2. Mix melted butter, milk, egg, and vanilla in a separate bowl.
3. Make an indentation in the middle of the dry ingredients, and pour in milk mixture. Mix until the batter is smooth.
4. Heat a lightly oiled pan over medium-high.
5. When pan is ready, pour approximately ¼ cup of batter per pancake, and cook until golden brown on each side.

Gluten Free Banana Pancakes with Cricket Protein

Prep time: 5 minutes
Cooking time: 3-5 minutes
Yield: 5 pancakes

Gluten Free Banana Pancakes with Cricket Protein

After we posted our recipe for our Cricket Flour Pancakes on our website at www.CricketFlours.com, we received a lot of requests for a gluten free recipe as well. This new recipe is a great alternative to use if you are looking for a gluten free pancake option. The combination of the banana, eggs, and almond milk provide the delicious flavors and base to the gluten free pancakes, and with the added protein and nutrition from the cricket protein. but one that still has that pancake consistency you love with added protein. The final pancake will be thinner than a normal pancake recipe, but will cook just the same for a great breakfast option that is high in protein and low in carbohydrates.

Ingredients:

- ∞ 2 bananas
- ∞ 2 eggs
- ∞ 1 tablespoon Cricket Flours: 100% Pure
- ∞ ¼ cup almond milk

Directions:

1. In a small mixing bowl add 1 1/2 banana, eggs, Cricket Flours: 100% Pure, and almond mix and whisk together until the mixture is fully combined.
2. Slice the remaining ½ banana and set to the side.
3. Using a lightly oiled frying pan brought to medium heat, add 1/3 cup of the mixture to the pan to begin cooking.
4. Cook until golden brown on both sides.
5. Remove from heat and add the sliced banana and any additional toppings as desired. Enjoy!

Spiced Granola with Cricket Flour

Prep time: 15 minutes
Cooking time: 35 minutes
Servings: 9-10

Spiced Granola with Cricket Flour

This spiced granola recipe is great for breakfast or with yogurt, and keeps well for snacks, hikes, etc. As you see from the ingredients below, we used currants, dates, apricots and peaches for the fruit. However, play around with your favorite dried fruits to create the perfect spiced granola that your family will love.

Ingredients:

- 4 cups oats
- 1 cup chopped pecans
- 1 cup shaved coconut
- 1 cup chopped almonds
- 2 ½ teaspoon cinnamon
- 1 teaspoon nutmeg
- ¹/₃ cup Cricket Flours: 100% Pure

- ½ cup butter
- ½ cup honey
- ¾ cup brown sugar
- ½ cup dried currants
- ½ cup dried dates
- ½ cup dried apricots
- ½ cup dried peaches

Directions:

1. Preheat oven to 335°F.
2. In a large bowl, mix oats, pecans, coconut, almonds, cinnamon, nutmeg, Cricket Flours: 100% Pure, and brown sugar.
3. Melt the butter in the microwave, and mix together with honey until fully blended. Pour mixture into the mixed oats and dry ingredients (no fruit).
4. Once mixed, spread out onto 2 non-stick baking sheets and place in the oven for 35 minutes. Every 7 minutes, mix and spread out the granola so that it fully crisps and does not burn.
5. Once golden brown, remove from the oven and let cool for 5 minutes before adding in the dried fruit.

Peanut Butter Protein Oatmeal

Cooking time: 5 minutes

Servings: 1

Peanut Butter Protein Oatmeal

Fresh berries and spices are some of our favorite ways to spice up our morning routines, but for this peanut butter protein oatmeal recipe we decided to do things a little differently. This recipe uses the rich flavor of peanut butter to carry this recipe, while combining chia seeds, coconut sugar, cricket protein, and oats for a delicious and protein packed morning dish.

Ingredients:

- ∞ ½ cup rolled oats
- ∞ 1 ¼ cups water
- ∞ ½ tablespoon chia seeds
- ∞ 1 tablespoon chunky peanut butter
- ∞ 1 tablespoon Cricket Flours: 100% Pure
- ∞ 1-2 tablespoons coconut sugar (sweeten to taste)

Directions:

1. In a small pot add together the 1 ¼ cups of water and rolled oats and set the heat to medium-high until boiling.
2. Next add the peanut butter and stir together with the oatmeal before removing the pot from heat.
3. Add in the chia seeds, cricket protein, and coconut sugar (sweeten to taste) and mix together until fully combined. Turn down the heat to medium and mix in the to boil

Bacon Infused Cheese Muffins

Prep time: 15 minutes
Cooking time: 18 minutes
Servings: 12

Bacon Infused Cheese Muffins

Take a break from the sweet stuff with this savory muffin recipe that's great for breakfast, brunch, or even dinner. Each muffin bakes with pieces of bacon and cheese that infuse each bite with their delicious flavors. Bacon, cheese, and nutritious cricket flour combine to keep you full through the morning. Eat one on your way to work or serve for brunch on the weekend.

Ingredients:

- 1 ½ cups baking flour
- ¼ cup Cricket Flours: 100% Pure
- ¼ cup sugar
- 1 ½ teaspoons baking powder
- 1 egg (beaten)
- ¾ cup milk
- $^{1}/_{3}$ cup oil (bacon drippings work best)
- ½ cup shredded sharp cheese
- 4 cooked bacon slices

Directions:

1. Preheat oven to 400°F.
2. Grease muffin tin lined with paper muffin cups.
3. In a medium mixing bowl combine flour, Cricket Flours: 100% Pure, sugar, baking powder.
4. In a separate bowl combine egg, milk, and oil.
5. Add egg mixture to dry ingredients, mixing only until just incorporated.
6. Slice bacon into small pieces, then add bacon and cheese to the muffin batter.
7. Spoon out the batter into muffin baking pan, and bake for 17-19 minutes. Toothpick or fork should come out clean.
8. 1 minute before removing from the oven, add a few small pieces of bacon and cheese for a flavorful and colorful topping.

Blueberry Cricket Protein Muffins

Prep time: 10 minutes
Cooking time: 15 minutes
Servings: 12

Blueberry Cricket Protein Muffins

A personal favorite and yearly tradition in my family, this blueberry muffin recipe fills your mouth with the taste of fresh picked blueberries. The savory combination of spices such as cinnamon, nutmeg, and added protein and nutrition from the cricket protein creates a great combination in this blueberry muffin recipe.

Ingredients:

- 1 ¼ cups all-purpose baking flour
- ¼ cup Cricket Flours: 100% Pure
- ¾ cup sugar
- 1 teaspoon baking powder
- ½ teaspoon salt
- ¼ teaspoon cinnamon
- ¼ teaspoon nutmeg
- 1 egg
- $^1/_3$ cup milk
- $^1/_3$ cup vegetable oil
- $^1/_3$ cup milk
- 1 ½ teaspoons vanilla extract
- 1 cup fresh/frozen blueberries

Directions:

1. Preheat oven to 400°F.
2. Grease muffin tin lined with paper muffin cups.
3. In a medium mixing bowl combine the dry ingredients.
4. In a separate bowl combine egg, milk, and oil.
5. Add the wet ingredients to dry ingredients, mixing only until just incorporated. Next fold in the fresh/frozen blueberries.
6. Spoon out the batter into muffin baking pan, and bake for 15 minutes. Toothpick or fork should come out clean.

Mini Lemon & Valencia Orange Raspberry Scones

Prep time: 15 minutes
Cooking time: 15 minutes
Servings: 24

Mini Lemon & Valencia Orange Raspberry Scones

This recipe is a delightful treat with fresh notes of lemon zest and Valencia oranges, coupled with fresh raspberries. Serve it with your favorite morning coffee or cappuccino, and savor this delicious scone recipe to start your morning off right.

Ingredients:

- ∞ 2 1/3 cups Cricket Flours All Purpose Baking Flour
- ∞ 1/3 cup sugar
- ∞ 2 teaspoons baking powder
- ∞ ¼ teaspoon baking soda
- ∞ ½ teaspoon salt
- ∞ 8 tablespoons frozen unsalted butter
- ∞ 1 large egg
- ∞ ½ cup Greek yogurt
- ∞ 1 tablespoon fresh squeezed lemon
- ∞ Zest of 1 lemon
- ∞ 1 ½ teaspoons Valencia orange peel
- ∞ 1 teaspoon vanilla extract
- ∞ 1 cup fresh raspberries

Directions:

1. Preheat oven to 400°F.
2. Lightly grease 2 muffin tins.
3. In a medium mixing bowl combine the sugar, orange peel, and lemon zest and mix together. Next add in the remaining Cricket Flours: All Purpose Baking Flour, baking powder, baking soda, and salt and mix until combined.
4. Grate frozen butter into the powder and mix until combined and the mixture is clumped.
5. In a separate bowl, mix the yogurt, egg, vanilla extract and lemon juice.
6. Gently fork in the liquid mix into the dry powder until combined, being careful to not over mix.
7. Gently fold in the fresh raspberries.
8. Spoon into muffin tins until halfway filled, and bake on the center rack of the oven for 15 minutes until golden brown.

PART
Two

Protein Shakes & Smoothies

Protein Shakes & Smoothies

These protein shakes and smoothies are some of our favorite creations that inspired us to launch our Cricket Flours products. They are great for breakfast, as a workout recovery drink, or a filling afternoon snack. Each of these recipes tastes delicious and can be individually customized to deliver the exact amount of protein and nutrition that YOU need and want. Happy blending!

Pineapple Raspberry Smoothie

Topical Tropical Protein Shake

Antioxidant Smoothie

Chocolate Covered Tart-Cherry Smoothie

Summer Lovin' Smoothie

Mango Cricket Protein Smoothie

Avocado Protein Smoothie

Strawberry Banana Smoothie

Pineapple Banana Protein Smoothie

Apple Pear Protein Smoothie

Frozen Cranberry Mango Smoothie with Cricket Protein

Cricket Dragon Smoothie

"It's so nice to be able to include my son in a healthy lifestyle with a tasty new protein shake that is natural, and safe for us both to enjoy! We love Cricket Flours!"

- **MaryPat & Benjamin**

Pineapple Raspberry Smoothie

Prep time: 10 minutes

Pineapple Raspberry Smoothie

This Pineapple Raspberry Smoothie is tantalizing combination of fresh tasting pineapple and raspberries with bright flavors to start your day! For this recipe we used our Cricket Fuel: Peruvian Chocolate single serve packs, but feel free to switch it up with our 100% Pure Original Flavor or Chocolate Peanut Butter as well!

Ingredients:

- ¾ cup pineapple juice
- 1 cup frozen raspberries
- 2 tablespoons Cricket Fuel: Peruvian Chocolate
- 1 fresh banana
- ½ cup ice

Directions:

1. Using a kitchen blender, first add together the pineapple juice, peeled banana, and Cricket Fuel: Peruvian Chocolate. Next add in the frozen raspberries and ice and blend all ingredients together on medium powder until smooth. Enjoy!

Topical Tropical Protein Shake

Prep time: 10 minutes

Topical Tropical Protein Shake

Maybe it's the dead of winter and you need a tropical escape. Or perhaps a poolside drink that does the body good. We've made it easy for you with frozen fruits and our natural source of protein. Whatever the occasion, this refreshing topical tropical protein shake is a great combination of some of our favorite fruits, mango and pineapple, but with a new twist…cricket protein!

Ingredients:

- 1 cup frozen mango
- ½ cup frozen pineapple
- 2 tablespoons Cricket Flours: 100% Pure
- 1 cup almond milk
- 1 teaspoon vanilla extract

Directions:

1. Using a kitchen blender, blend together Cricket Flours: 100% Pure and almond milk.
2. Add in the frozen fruit and vanilla.
3. On medium power, blend all ingredients until smooth.
4. Serve with a tiny umbrella and a hula-style shake of the hips.

Antioxidant Smoothie

Prep time: 5 minutes

Antioxidant Smoothie

This antioxidant smoothie is a healthy combination of frozen strawberries, cherries, pomegranate seeds, blueberries, and red raspberries for a boost of nutrients and protein from our Cricket Flours: 100% Pure. With 10g of cricket protein, and a delicious blend of fruits packed with antioxidants, this smoothie is a real treat!

Ingredients:

- ¼ cup frozen strawberries
- ¼ cup frozen cherries
- ¼ cup frozen pomegranate seeds
- ¼ cup frozen blueberries
- ¼ cup frozen red raspberries
- 2 tablespoons Cricket Flours: 100% Pure
- 1 cup coconut milk
- 1 banana

Directions:

2. Using a kitchen blender, first add together the coconut milk, peeled banana, and Cricket Flours: 100% Pure. Next add in the frozen fruit and blend all ingredients together on medium powder until smooth. Enjoy!

Chocolate Covered Tart-Cherry Smoothie

Prep time: 10 minutes

Chocolate Covered Tart-Cherry Smoothie

We love puckering up to tart cherries and decided to experiment with one of our favorite smoothie flavors, adding Cricket Flours: 100% Pure for protein and nutrients, of course. This smoothie combines a tart taste from the cherries with a hint of chocolate from the cocoa powder to make a smoothie on the savory side. Serve this one to your sweetheart and they'll love you forever.

Ingredients:

- ∞ 1 cup frozen dark tart cherries
- ∞ 2 tablespoons Cricket Flours: 100% Pure
- ∞ 1 ¼ cups almond milk
- ∞ 1 teaspoon vanilla extract
- ∞ 1 ½ teaspoons cocoa powder
- ∞ ½ cup ice

Directions:

1. In a blender, combine frozen cherries, cricket protein, and cocoa powder.
2. Next, add in ice, vanilla, and almond milk, and blend until smooth.

Summer Lovin' Smoothie

Prep time: 10 minutes

Summer Lovin' Smoothie

Summertime is the best time for peaches, blackberries, and strawberries. Freeze your own fruits from the farmer's market, or buy frozen when you need a wintertime pick-me-up. The fresh taste and fruit-filled flavor in this smoothie is perfect for a summer afternoon or a tasty drink at all times of the year. If you have the fortune to enjoy this on the beach, just remember to send me a postcard.

Ingredients:

- ∞ 1 cup frozen peaches
- ∞ ½ cup frozen blackberries
- ∞ ½ cup frozen strawberries
- ∞ 2 tablespoons Cricket Flours: 100% Pure
- ∞ 1 cup almond milk

Directions:

1. In a blender, add frozen peaches, blackberries, strawberries, and cricket protein together.
2. Pour in 1 cup almond milk and blend until smooth.

Mango Cricket Protein Smoothie

Prep time: 5 minutes

Mango Cricket Protein Smoothie

While fresh sliced mango ranks at the top of my list of favorite fruits, this mango smoothie comes in at a close second. This simple smoothie only uses a handful of ingredients to craft a smooth combination of mango, coconut milk, and Greek yogurt for a perfect smoothie.

Ingredients:

- ∞ 1 cup frozen mango
- ∞ 2/3 cup coconut milk
- ∞ ½ cup Greek yogurt
- ∞ ½ cup ice
- ∞ 2 tablespoons Cricket Flours: 100% Pure (or 1 Cricket Fuel pack)
- ∞ 1 cup almond milk

Directions:

1. In a blender add together all of the ingredients and blend until smooth. Enjoy!

Avocado Protein Smoothie

Prep time: 5 minutes

Avocado Protein Smoothie

This avocado protein smoothie packs a healthy punch of protein, healthy fats (oleic acid), over 14 types of minerals, fiber and more! While visiting with some family friends from Brazil, we started sharing our favorite recipes and decided to create a new rendition of a popular smoothie flavor from Sao Paulo, Brazil. With only a few ingredients, this smooth protein and nutrient dense smoothie is a great morning or afternoon treat!

Ingredients:

- 2 ripe avocados
- 1 cup coconut milk
- 2 tablespoons clover honey
- 2 tablespoons Cricket Flours: 100% Pure (or 1 Cricket Fuel pack)

Directions:

1. In a blender add together all of the ingredients and blend until smooth. Enjoy!

Strawberry Banana Smoothie

Prep time: 10 minutes

Strawberry Banana Smoothie

If it ain't broke, don't fix it. The Strawberry Banana Smoothie brings your taste buds back to the basics using summer strawberries, fresh bananas, and Cricket Flours: 100% Pure. This is the ultimate quick meal, using only four ingredients. Besides being speedy-quick to make, this smoothie is also a great source of potassium, vitamin C, B12, B5, protein, and more.

Ingredients:

- ∞ 1 cup frozen strawberries
- ∞ 1 banana
- ∞ 2 tablespoons Cricket Flours: 100% Pure
- ∞ 1 cup almond milk

Directions:

1. In a blender, add frozen strawberries, banana, and pure cricket protein together.
2. Next, pour in 1 cup almond milk and blend until smooth.

Pineapple Banana Protein Smoothie

Prep time: 10 minutes

Pineapple Banana Protein Smoothie

This recipe is fresh take on one of my favorite smoothie recipes. By using fresh mint leaves, coupled with classic flavors such as pineapple, banana, almonds, creates a refreshing combination of flavors to fuel your next workout or adventure.

Ingredients:

- ∞ 1 frozen banana
- ∞ ½ cup frozen pineapple chunks
- ∞ ¾ cup almond milk
- ∞ 2 tablespoons Cricket Flours: 100% Pure
- ∞ 4 fresh mint leaves

Directions:

1. In a standard kitchen blender add together all the ingredients and blend together until smooth.

Apple Pear Protein Smoothie

Prep time: 10 minutes

Apple Pear Protein Smoothie

As some of our followers from our social media accounts and live events know, we often incorporate fresh ingredients in our recipes whenever available. For this Apple Pear Protein Smoothie we used fresh pears and apples that were picked ripe and straight from our garden to add a crisp taste and texture to this new smoothie!

Ingredients:

- ∞ 1 sliced apple
- ∞ 1 sliced pear
- ∞ ½ cup Greek yogurt
- ∞ 2 tablespoons Cricket Flours: 100% Pure
- ∞ ¼ cup ice
- ∞ 1 teaspoon cinnamon

Directions:

1. In a standard kitchen blender add together all the ingredients and blend together until smooth.

Frozen Cranberry Mango Smoothie with Cricket Protein

Prep time: 10 minutes

Frozen Cranberry Mango Smoothie with Cricket Protein

The Frozen Cranberry Mango Smoothie with added cricket protein is a great fall fruit smoothie that truly hits the spot. In addition to our Cricket Flours: 100% Pure this recipe features frozen cranberries, red grapes, mango, vanilla Greek yogurt, and coconut milk. Coupled with the bright notes of cranberry and grape, this fruit smoothie is a great source of calcium, fiber, and vitamin C from each of the all natural ingredients. Because we use cricket protein in our smoothies, they are naturally a good source of iron, B12, Omega-3s, Omega-6s, and it contains all the essential amino acids as well. To make your own Frozen Cranberry Mango Smoothie with Cricket Flours, check out the following ingredients and directions below. Enjoy!

Ingredients:

- ∞ 1/3 cup frozen cranberries
- ∞ 2/3 cup frozen red grapes
- ∞ 2/3 cup frozen mango
- ∞ ½ cup Greek Yogurt
- ∞ 1 cup coconut milk
- ∞ 2 tablespoons Cricket Flours: 100% Pure

Directions:

1. In a standard kitchen blender add together all the ingredients and blend together until smooth.

Cricket Dragon Smoothie

Prep time: 10 minutes

Cricket Dragon Smoothie

Who doesn't want to try a Cricket Dragon Smoothie? This smoothie is made with frozen Pitaya, or also known as dragon fruit, and a mixture of mango, pineapple juice and our Cricket Fuel: Peruvian Chocolate flavor!

Ingredients:

- ∞ ¾ cup frozen pitaya/dragon fruit
- ∞ 1 cup frozen mango slices
- ∞ Cricket Fuel: Peruvian Chocolate (1 packet)
- ∞ ¾ cup pineapple juice

Directions:

1. In a standard kitchen blender add together all the ingredients and blend together until smooth.

PART
Three

Salads & Sauces

Salads & Sauces

Now you can harness the power of our Cricket Flours in your lunchtime salads and old family recipe of Fettuccine Alfredo. Making your own salad dressing is quick and easy, and you probably have all of the ingredients on hand already. It's also a good way to avoid the additives and artificial ingredients sometimes found in bottled dressings. Since launching our business, we have experimented with thousands of different combinations to create delicious recipes and products. As we imagined the possibilities of how our cricket powder could be used, we knew we wanted to find a way to incorporate it in sauces and vegetable dishes. These salad dressings and sauces are a delicious surprise for not only yours truly, but now your taste buds, too. If you want extra salad dressing on hand, double the recipe of your choice and keep covered in the refrigerator for up to a week. The olive oil with solidify when cold, so take the dressing out of the fridge thirty minutes before your stomach starts grumbling.

Pomegranate Toasted Cashew Mixed Green Salad

Lemon Dressing

Mustard Dressing

Sweet Lemon Balsamic Vinaigrette

Alfredo Sauce

Balsamic Fig Dressing/Sauce

"It's been on my "To Do" list for quite some time to be able to use cricket flour as part of my daily protein intake, and now I'm lucky enough to do so! There's no denying the sustainability of cricket flour and that means so much to me as a consumer. Better for the environment and delicious? Sign me up!"

- Anne Haugaard

Pomegranate Toasted Cashew Mixed Green Salad

Prep time: 7 minutes

Pomegranate Toasted Cashew Mixed Green Salad

Caesar and the Chef can't hold a candle to this powerhouse of a salad. Crunchy pomegranate seeds and toasted cashews contribute great textures and flavors to classic mixed greens. We especially like this salad with our Sweet Lemon Balsamic Vinaigrette. This salad can stand alone or play a supporting role to Bacon Creamed Chicken for dinner. Toast cashews in the oven at 400°F for 5-10 minutes, or in the microwave for 3-5 minutes.

Ingredients:

- 1 ½ cups mixed greens
- 1 ½ tablespoons pomegranate seeds
- 1 tablespoon toasted cashews
- 1 tablespoon salad dressing

- (Optional) Cheese crumbles of your choice, such as feta, blue, or goat cheese.

Directions:

1. On a plate or in a bowl, add mixed greens, toasted cashews, and pomegranate seeds. Add cheese, if using.
2. Toss with your favorite salad dressing, or use one of our recipes such as our Sweet Lemon Balsamic Vinaigrette or Mustard Dressing.

Lemon Dressing

Prep time: 5 minutes

Lemon Dressing

Citrus and salad greens were meant for each other. The bright acidity of the lemon makes a humble green leaf simply sing. With garlic and cilantro, too, you've got one heck of a dressing. A salad with this dressing would pair wonderfully with an entrée of fish or chicken. Lemon is the star here, so if you want less of a zing, sweeten to taste with honey.

Ingredients:

- ∞ 3 tablespoons extra virgin olive oil
- ∞ 3 tablespoons fresh lemon juice
- ∞ 1 teaspoon Cricket Flours: 100% Pure
- ∞ ½ teaspoon fresh cilantro
- ∞ ½ teaspoon minced garlic

Directions:

1. In a small mixing bowl, add in all ingredients and whisk together until fully mixed. Enjoy!

Mustard Dressing

Prep time: 5 minutes

Mustard Dressing

Any sandwich made with a quality mustard is a winner in my book. What better way to make your mustard multitask than including it in a salad dressing? The classic honey mustard dressing gets an updated health profile with cricket powder. If you really want to impress your taste buds or dinner guests, serve this on a salad topped with pork tenderloin. Make plenty for second helpings.

Ingredients:

- ∞ 3 tablespoons extra virgin olive oil
- ∞ 2 tablespoons cider vinegar
- ∞ 1 teaspoon prepared mustard
- ∞ 1 teaspoon Cricket Flours: 100% Pure
- ∞ 2 teaspoon honey

Directions:

1. In a small mixing bowl, add in all ingredients and whisk together until fully mixed. Enjoy!

Sweet Lemon Balsamic Vinaigrette Dressing

Prep time: 5 minutes

Sweet Lemon Balsamic Vinaigrette Dressing

This cricket protein recipe is guaranteed to be a new family favorite in your kitchen. Sweet Lemon Balsamic Vinaigrette is a great combination of balsamic vinegar and fresh lemon juice. We temper the acidity of the lemon and vinegar with honey and olive oil to create a balanced dressing that goes perfectly with…well, everything!

Ingredients:

- ∞ 3 tablespoons extra virgin olive oil
- ∞ 2 tablespoons fresh lemon juice
- ∞ 1 tablespoon balsamic vinegar
- ∞ 3 teaspoon honey
- ∞ 1 teaspoon Cricket Flours: 100% Pure
- ∞ ½ teaspoon minced garlic
- ∞ 1 pinch Italian seasoning

Directions:

1. In a small mixing bowl, add in all ingredients and whisk together until fully mixed.

Alfredo Sauce

Cooking time: 8 minutes
Servings: 6-8

Alfredo Sauce

Oh, the blessed Alfredo Sauce! No longer need you rely upon your neighborhood Italian spot to deliver this rich and creamy delight. And with cricket powder added, you just might be able to convince yourself that this is the new health food. We also like the addition of cream cheese to our Alfredo for a little tang. Think outside the pasta box and serve this sauce alongside your next steak dinner, or ladle it on top of asparagus or broccoli as we did in the appetizer section.

Ingredients:

- ∞ 1 teaspoon butter
- ∞ 2 cloves garlic
- ∞ 1 tablespoon all-purpose flour
- ∞ 1 $^1/_3$ cups skim milk

- ∞ 2 tablespoons cream cheese
- ∞ 1 ¼ cups grated parmesan cheese
- ∞ 2 teaspoons Cricket Flours: 100% Pure

Directions:

1. In a food processor, blend milk and cricket powder until fully mixed.
2. Use a medium sauce pan to make the roux: combine butter, garlic, all-purpose flour, and cricket powder milk mixture. Stir constantly on medium heat for 3-4 minutes until thickened.
3. Add both the cream cheese parmesan, and continuing stirring until cheese is fully melted.

Balsamic Fig Dressing/Sauce

Prep time: 10 minutes

Servings: 12-15

Balsamic Fig Dressing/Sauce

Balsamic Fig Dressing/Sauce is an old family recipe that tastes wonderfully on fish, chicken, beef, and salads. The combination of oranges, balsamic vinegar, and figs with transport you straight to the Mediterranean coast. Your family and friends will be begging you for the recipe. Enjoy their looks of surprise when you tell them the secret ingredient is cricket powder!

Ingredients:

- 3 tablespoons fresh orange juice
- 1 tablespoon orange zest
- ½ cup balsamic vinegar
- $^1/_3$ cup diced dried figs
- 1 cup extra virgin olive oil
- 1 tablespoon Cricket Flours: 100% Pure
- 1 tablespoon diced shallots
- ½ teaspoon vanilla extract
- ¼ teaspoon salt
- 1 tablespoon water

Directions:

1. In a food processor, combine all ingredients except for the olive oil. Start processor on low, slowly increasing to medium for 1 minute.
2. Next, set the processor back to low and gradually pour in 1 cup of olive oil. Continue processing until dried figs are fully mixed in and sauce is smooth.
3. Once smooth, pour into a serving dish or dipping tray.

PART
Four

Appetizers

Appetizers

When you need to create a three-course meal or a dish to contribute to the next potluck or Super Bowl Party, look no further. Combine these recipes with your other favorite small plates for a fun tapas-style dinner, too. Both of these recipes deliver a complex profile of flavors that are not only nutritious, but are sure to be the conversation piece of any event.

Alfredo Baked Broccoli

Sour Cream Cricket Cheesy Dip

Spicy Baked Peppers

Caramelized Maple Baked Brussels Sprouts

Fresh Applesauce with Cricket Protein

Chocolate Covered Cricket Strawberries

Cricket Stuffed Snow Peas

"Sooooo much yum yum in my tum tum."

- **Matthew Gurnick**

Alfredo Baked Broccoli

Prep time: 15 minutes
Cooking time: 15 minutes
Yield: 6 servings

Alfredo Baked Broccoli

Alfredo Baked Broccoli combines our delicious Alfredo Sauce recipe found previously with baked broccoli. A vitamin-packed dark green vegetable and indulgent Alfredo Sauce—this is the power couple of appetizers. This dish is best served hot and would also be a great side dish for your next meal.

Ingredients:

- ∞ 4 cups broccoli florets
- ∞ ½ teaspoon minced garlic
- ∞ $^1/_3$ cup olive oil
- ∞ Alfredo Sauce

Directions:

1. Preheat oven to 400°F.
2. Rinse broccoli and spread out florets on a baking sheet.
3. In a small bowl, combine olive oil and minced garlic and drizzle lightly over the broccoli.
4. Bake for 15 minutes until lightly browned.
5. Ladle hot Alfredo Sauce over baked broccoli and serve immediately.

Sour Cream Cricket Cheesy Dip

Prep time: 10 minutes

Yield: 12 servings

Sour Cream Cricket Cheesy Dip

Getting ready for the big game? Or planning an upcoming dinner party or event? This Sour Cream Cricket Cheesy Dip is the perfect dipping sauce packed with your herbs, cheeses, and flavor. This recipe is easy to put together, and a great way to prep for your event and set in the refrigerator to chill until your guests arrive to kick off the party!

Ingredients:

- 8 oz sour cream
- 8 oz cream cheese
- ½ tablespoon minced garlic
- $^1/_3$ cup green onion
- 1 teaspoon cilantro
- ½ teaspoon cumin
- 1 cup shredded cheddar cheese
- ½ oz dry ranch salad dressing mix
- 1 diced tomatoes
- ½ tablespoon Cricket Flours: 100% Pure
- 1 diced jalapeno pepper

Directions:

1. In a medium mixing bowl, mix all of the ingredients and chill for 2 hours before serving. Serve with a mix of tortilla chips and enjoy!

Spicy Baked Peppers

Prep time: 7 minutes
Cooking time: 20 minutes
Yield: 10 servings

Spicy Baked Peppers

The ultimate party food appetizer. These spicy baked peppers feature a spicy combination of four cheeses, chili powder, white pepper, red pepper flakes and cricket protein. These can easily be sliced into smaller, bite-size pieces that would be great for a party platter.

Ingredients:

- 5 Anaheim peppers
- 2 cups four-cheese blend
- 2 teaspoons Cricket Flours: 100% Pure
- 1 egg
- ¼ teaspoon chili powder
- $^1/_8$ teaspoon white pepper
- 1 pinch of salt
- 2 teaspoons red pepper flakes

Directions:

1. Preheat oven to 375°F. Grease a large baking pan or cookie sheet.
2. Rinse peppers and slice down the length of each pepper. Remove all seeds.
3. In a mixing bowl, mix cheese, egg, cricket powder, salt, chili powder, and white pepper.
4. Using a spoon, spread cheese mixture into the cavity of each pepper. Sprinkle red pepper flakes on top.
5. Place peppers on baking pan and bake in the oven for 20 minutes. Serve warm.

Caramelized Maple Baked Brussels Sprouts

Prep time: 5 minutes
Cooking time: 35 minutes
Yield: 5 servings

Caramelized Maple Baked Brussels Sprouts

For current Brussels sprouts fans and those still on the fence, this maple twist is a true delight! Brussels sprouts are naturally a great source of Vitamin C, A, B-6, and coupled with cricket protein and maple syrup are a great appetizer for your next meal.

Ingredients:

- 2 cups halved Brussels sprouts
- 4 tablespoons virgin olive oil
- 3 tablespoons pure maple syrup
- 1 teaspoon Cricket Flours: 100% Pure
- 1 pinch salt
- 1 pinch pepper

Directions:

1. Preheat oven to 400°F.
2. Rinse and halve 2 cups Brussels sprouts and mix together in a medium mixing bowl with the olive oil, maple syrup, cricket powder, salt, and pepper.
3. Line a baking sheet or cookie pan with aluminum foil and spread the Brussels sprouts mixture evenly on the sheet.
4. Place the baking sheet on the center rack of the oven and bake for 35 minutes or until the Brussels sprouts are golden brown.

Fresh Applesauce with Cricket Protein

Prep time: 5 minutes
Cooking time: 35 minutes
Yield: 5 servings

Fresh Applesauce with Cricket Protein

For this Fresh Applesauce recipe with cricket protein we used farm-fresh apples, pears, and cinnamon to create a dish that is great for a chilly fall evening when warm and fresh, or as a refreshing treat when served chilled.

Ingredients:

- 8 sliced apples
- 2 sliced pears olive oil
- 3 ½ cups water
- ¼ cup Cricket Flours: 100% Pure
- 1 ½ teaspoons cinnamon

Directions:

1. Using a cutting board start preparing the applesauce recipe by slicing the apples and pears into small pieces. We prefer to keep the skins on for additional nutrients, but feel free to peel them as well.
2. Set the stovetop to high and add the sliced apples, pears and water to a standard cooking pot and cover the pot to bring to a rolling boil.
3. Once boiling, reduce the heat to low and let the mixture simmer for 45 minutes while stirring occasionally.
4. After the apples and pears have fully cooked down, add in the cinnamon and cricket protein, and stir until fully combined.

Chocolate Covered Cricket Strawberries

Prep time: 10 minutes
Cooking time: 10 minutes
Yield: 30 servings

Chocolate Covered Cricket Strawberries

At a recent museum event, we were asked to put together fresh appetizer and treat using our cricket protein. The chocolate covered cricket strawberries truly hit the mark by creating a dish with fresh local fruit, is easy to share, and great opportunity for people to try edible insects for a sustainable alternative protein!

Ingredients:

- ∞ 12 oz semi-sweet chocolate chips
- ∞ 6 oz classic white chips
- ∞ 1lb fresh strawberries
- ∞ 1 tablespoon Cricket Flours: 100% Pure

Directions:

1. Using a double boiler, set the water temperature to gently simmering, and place the semi-sweet chocolate chips into the center unit. Stir constantly until fully melted. Slowly add in the Cricket Flours: 100% Pure until fully combined.
2. Remove from heat and dip washed strawberries in the melted chocolate, and set on a parchment or tin foil lined surface.
3. Using a clean double boiler, repeat the process with the classic white chips until melted, but without the added cricket protein. Once melted, use a fork to drizzle and decorate the strawberries.
4. Chill the strawberries to cool and set the chocolate. Enjoy!

Cricket Stuffed Snow Peas

Prep time: 15 minutes
Cooking time: 30 seconds
Yield: 15 servings

Cricket Stuffed Snow Peas

Looking for a new twist to add to your delicious summer harvest of snow peas? This Cricket Stuffed Snow Pea recipe is a fun way to use fresh snow peas in a new way with the piped cricket stuffing to really step up your appetizer plating and flair.

Ingredients:

- 30 snow peas
- 4 tablespoons of butter (room temperature)
- 16 oz cream cheese (room temperature)
- 2 tablespoons minced garlic
- 1 tablespoon chopped basil
- 1 tablespoon Cricket Flours: 100% Pure
- 1 teaspoon cracked black pepper
- 2 tablespoons chopped chives
- 1 ½ tablespoons minced parsley leaves
- ½ teaspoon sea salt
- 1 tablespoon fresh lemon juice

Directions:

1. In a medium sized mixing bowl, add together all of the ingredients except for the snow peas and lemon juice, and mix until combined.
2. Once combined, add the mixture to a piping bag or large plastic storage bag with a small cut made to a corner and set aside.
3. Bring a medium sized pan of lightly salted water to boil, and blanch snow peas for about 30 seconds and then pat dry. (To blanch, you will want to place the snow peas in the boiling water for 30 seconds, and then drop them in a bowl of icy water before patting them dry.)
4. Use a small knife to slice and split the peas along the curved side to open.
5. Pipe in the mixture from your bag, and finish them off by adding a light drizzle of fresh lemon juice. Enjoy!

PART
Five

Entrées

Entrées

Dinner is served! In our cookbook, "All Cricket, No BULL…" we decided to create recipes using our Cricket Flours products not just as source of protein for smoothies and sauces. Because of the versatility of cricket powder, we like to add nutrition wherever we can, and entrées are no exception. While the main ingredients of both of these entrées are already a great source of protein, these recipes use Cricket Flours to add additional nutrition and flavors to each and every plate.

Bacon Creamed Chicken

Cricket Meat Tacos

Baked Lemon Chicken

Sautéed Salmon with Balsamic Fig Dipping Sauce

Cricket Pizza

"I've been waiting for something like Cricket Flour for a long time. I love backpacking and this stuff is not only delicious, it is a great source of protein and carbs at a light weight. Perfect for powering though a long day on the trail!"

- Alexis John

Bacon Creamed Chicken

Prep time: 20 minutes

Cooking time: 3 hours

Servings: 8

Bacon Creamed Chicken

Everything's better with bacon… and Cricket Flours, might we add. Perfect for a hands-off, weeknight meal, Bacon Creamed Chicken is your next most popular request. Have no fear of serving a dry bird with this dish. Wrapped in bacon, cooked on top of corn beef, and covered in a coconut crème sauce, Bacon Creamed Chicken is moist and flavorful. Serve over jasmine rice or vegetables for a complete meal.

Ingredients:

- ∞ 8 chicken breasts
- ∞ 8 pieces of bacon
- ∞ ¼ lb corned beef
- ∞ 8oz sour cream

- ∞ 14oz can coconut cream
- ∞ ¼ cup Cricket Flours: 100% Pure
- ∞ 6 tablespoons cooking sherry
- ∞ 2 cups sliced whole mushrooms

Directions:

1. Preheat oven to 275°F.
2. In a glass pan, slice pieces of corned beef and cover the bottom with a layer of beef.
3. Wrap each chicken breast with a piece of bacon and place in the glass pan.
4. In medium mixing bowl, mix together sour cream, coconut cream, cricket powder, and cooking sherry.
5. Spoon and spread cream mixture over bacon wrapped chicken and cover pan with aluminum foil.
6. Set the pan in the oven and cook for 3 hours.
7. After 2 hours of cooking, remove aluminum foil and sprinkle mushrooms on top of the cooking chicken for the last hour.

Cricket Meat Tacos

Prep time: 10 minutes
Cooking time: 40 minutes
Servings: 5

Cricket Meat Tacos

So many of our recipes use cricket protein in new ways for smoothies, baked goods, and more but we really wanted to create another great go to dinner option. This Cricket Meat Taco recipe is an easy way to throw together some delicious ingredients and cricket protein for a dish that really hits the spot with a nice spicy finish!

Ingredients:

- ∞ 1 lb ground beef
- ∞ 1 fresh medium yellow onion
- ∞ 1 ½ teaspoon cayenne powder
- ∞ 1 fresh diced red tomato
- ∞ 1 diced jalapeno pepper
- ∞ 1 teaspoon basil
- ∞ 1 teaspoon oregano

- ∞ 2 teaspoons minced garlic
- ∞ ½ teaspoon salt
- ∞ ½ teaspoon crushed black pepper
- ∞ 1/3 cup water
- ∞ 3 tablespoons Cricket Flours: 100% Pure

Directions:

1. In a medium pan, sauté the ground beef, onion and garlic on medium heat.
2. Turn the heat to low, and add in the remaining ingredients while stirring until completely combined and mixed in.
3. Cover and let simmer for 10-15 minutes until the water is absorbed.
4. Use taco shells and your favorite taco toppings to create a delicious Cricket Meat Taco! Enjoy!

Baked Lemon Chicken

Prep time: 5 minutes
Cooking time: 40-45 minutes
Servings: 2-3

Baked Lemon Chicken

Try this new cricket protein infused baked lemon chicken recipe! We wanted to create a simple recipe that was packed with flavors, easy to make, and infused with amazing flavors. Easily customize your own recipe by adding in your favorite garden fresh vegetables and more!

Ingredients:

- 8 chicken tenders
- ¼ cup diced green peppers
- 2 sliced baby red potatoes
- 1 teaspoon minced garlic
- 1 pinch sea salt
- 1 pinch pepper
- 1 fresh lemon
- 2 teaspoons Cricket Flours: 100% Pure

Directions:

1. Preheat oven to 350°F.
2. Using a cutting board, slice green peppers and baby red potatoes, and cut ½ of the lemon into small strips.
3. Take two strips of aluminum foil to create pouches and add in the sliced vegetables, lemon strips and minced garlic.
4. Mix together the Cricket Flours: 100% Pure, salt, and pepper and add on top of the vegetables and lemon mixture.
5. Next place 4 chicken tenders on top and pinch close the top of the aluminum foil pouches.
6. Place the pouches on a baking sheet and place on the center rack of the oven for 35 minutes.
7. After 35 minutes, open the top of the pouches, and bake for an additional 5 minutes while exposed.
8. Remove from the oven and plate with a cooked mixture of brown rice, red rice, and black barley for a delicious meal.
9. Finish off the dish by using the fresh lemon juice from ½ lemon and enjoy!

Sautéed Salmon with Balsamic Fig Dipping Sauce

Prep time: 12 minutes
Cooking time: 13-15 minutes
Servings: 2

Sautéed Salmon with Balsamic Fig Dipping Sauce

Living near the Oregon coast, we have great access to fresh fish from local fisherman, such as the salmon pictured for this recipe. If you don't live near a coastline, use this recipe as an excuse to visit your local fishmonger. This recipe is chock-full of healthy fats from the fish and coconut oil, and tarragon is our personal favorite addition to salmon. To top it off, we combined this recipe with our Balsamic Fig Sauce that makes a delicious pairing.

Ingredients:

- ∞ 2 salmon fillets
- ∞ 2 tablespoons coconut oil
- ∞ 1 pinch of salt
- ∞ 1 pinch of tarragon

Directions:

1. In a frying pan or cast-iron skillet set on medium-low heat, add coconut oil to melt and coat the bottom of the pan.
2. When oil is heated, add both salmon fillets with the scales on the bottom and sprinkle with salt and tarragon.
3. Cover the pan and cook for 13-15 minutes, being careful not to overcook.
4. The center should be moist and light pink. Once done, plate each fillet and add your Balsamic Fig Dipping sauce.

Cricket Pizza

Prep time: 20 minutes
Cooking time: 15-18 minutes
Servings: 8

Cricket Pizza

We love getting the family together, and customizing our own pizzas is so much fun! Do you love specialty cheeses? Spinach? Meatlovers? Pineapple? Add them all and create your own delicious Cricket Pizza using this cricket protein dough recipe for added protein and nutrition.

Ingredients:

- ∞ 1 active dry yeast package
- ∞ 1 teaspoon sugar
- ∞ 1 cup warm water
- ∞ 2 cups bread flour
- ∞ ½ cup Cricket Flours: 100% Pure
- ∞ 2 tablespoons virgin olive oil
- ∞ 1 teaspoon sea salt

Directions:

1. Preheat oven to 450°F.
2. In a mixing bowl, combine the warm water, sugar, and active dry yeast and stir until dissolved. Let stand for 10 minutes.
3. Stir in the bread flour, Cricket Flours: 100% Pure, sea salt, and olive oil and mix until smooth. Let the mixture sit for 5-8 minutes (Mixture can be left covered in a warm location for 45-60 minutes for a thicker crust).
4. Turn dough out on a lightly floured bread board and knead 1 to 2 times before using.
5. Add on your favorite pizza toppings bake on the center rack of the oven for 15-20 minutes. Enjoy!

PART

Six

Desserts

Desserts

Most people don't think of desserts as being nutritious, but we know better. Each of our desserts includes healthful ingredients such as dark chocolate, ginger, strawberries, and, of course, Cricket Flours. When we first started testing our new recipes, we knew that these desserts were sure to win over people's tastebuds. Although many people may not have tried cricket protein before, we knew that they would love the taste of our Cinnamon Baked Apple, Hazelnut Liquor Cake, and Dark Molasses Ginger Snap Cookies. When your day needs a sweet ending, look right here.

Cricket Flour Brownies

Triple Layer Brownies

Hazelnut Liquor Cake

Double Chocolate Cricket Crispies

Strawberry Chocolate Ice Cream Shake

Cinnamon Baked Apple

"Lemony Cricket" Pudding Cake

Dark Molasses Ginger Snap Cookies

Peanut Butter Chocolate Chip Cookies

"Not only do I think Cricket Flours is a great idea, but I have been fortunate enough to try the product already in brownie form. Delicious! Not only are Cricket Flours products tasty and healthy, but good for our environment. It is a win all around! I look forward to supporting their products in the future."

- Jordan Bailey

Cricket Flour Brownies

Prep time: 30 minutes
Cooking time: 24 minutes
Yield: 8inch-by-8inch pan

Cricket Flour Brownies

The Cricket Flour Brownie is one of the first recipes we made using our Cricket Flours: All-Purpose Baking Flour. This is a family recipe I have used since I was a kid, and it is simple and delicious. Just remember to not overheat your chocolate and butter as they are melting, and only add in the egg once the mixture has slightly cooled. Serve a la mode with your favorite vanilla or mint ice cream.

Ingredients:

- ½ cup butter
- 6 tablespoons cocoa
- pinch of salt
- 1 teaspoons vanilla
- 2 eggs
- 1 cup sugar
- ¾ cup Cricket Flours: All Purpose Baking Flour

Directions:

1. Preheat oven to 350°F. Grease an 8x8 inch baking pan.
2. On low heat, melt butter in a medium saucepan, then mix in cocoa and salt. Take off heat.
3. Add in the sugar, Cricket Flours: All Purpose Baking Flour, eggs, vanilla, and mix until smooth.
4. Pour the mixed batter into prepared pan.
5. Bake for 24 minutes.
6. Check doneness with a toothpick. It should come out clean. The cricket flour brownies may not look fully done, but they will continue to cook once removed. You do not want to overcook your delicious cricket flour brownies.

Triple Layer Brownies

Prep time: 15 minutes
Cooking time: 20-25 minutes
Yield: 8inch-by-8inch pan

Triple Layer Brownies

Who doesn't love brownies? We do so much we launched a Kickstarter raising over $25K for our new brownie mix, and put together this new triple layer brownie recipe with Crickets!

Ingredients:

- 16oz can chocolate syrup
- 4 eggs
- 3 cups powdered sugar
- 1 cup granulated sugar
- 1 cup all purpose baking flour
- 1 cup softened butter
- 1/3 cup Cricket Flours: Peruvian Chocolate
- 2oz semi sweet bakers chocolate
- 4 tablespoons milk
- 2 tablespoons vanilla extract

Directions:

1. Preheat oven to 350°F. Grease an 8x8 inch baking pan.
2. In a standard kitchen mixer, combine 8oz softened butter, 1 cup sugar, 1 tablespoon vanilla, and Cricket Flours: Peruvian Chocolate and mix on slow-medium speed. Add the mixture to the baking pan and set on the center rack of the over for 20-25minutes until fully cooked.
3. For the icing layer, begin with 6 tablespoons melted butter and 1 tablespoon vanilla in a kitchen mixer. Slowly add in the powdered sugar and milk while alternating between the two. Add food coloring for any desired color, and begin icing the brownies once cooled.
4. For the third and final layer, melt 2oz semi sweet bakers chocolate and 3 tablespoons of butter in a small sauce pan set on low heat. Once melted, slowly drizzle the mixture on top of the iced brownies to finish off your delicious triple layer brownies.

Hazelnut Liquor Cake

Prep time: 20 minutes
Cooking time: 60 minutes
Yield: 12-14 servings

Hazelnut Liquor Cake

The Hazelnut Liquor Cake is a fluffy and delicious cake with hints of sweet hazelnut. The recipe uses our Cricket Flours: 100% Pure to add additional protein and nutty flavor that pairs perfectly with the hazelnut. We recommend that you begin to make your glaze in the last 10 minutes of baking so that it can be added while the cake is still warm. This cake is worthy of a birthday or anniversary celebration, and needs nothing more than a glass of milk alongside it.

Ingredients:

- 2 $^2/_3$ cup all-purpose flour
- $^1/_3$ cup Cricket Flours: 100% Pure
- 1 teaspoon baking powder
- 2 cups sugar
- ½ cup vegetable oil
- 4 eggs
- ½ cup water
- ½ cup hazelnut liquor
- ½ cup milk
- ½ cup chopped hazelnuts
- 1 package instant vanilla pudding

Hazelnut Liquor Cake Directions:

1. Preheat oven to 350°F. Grease and lightly flour a bundt pan, shaking out excess flour.
2. With an electric mixer, carefully combine flour, cricket powder, sugar, baking powder, and instant vanilla pudding mix.
3. Add in vegetable oil, eggs, hazelnut liquor, and milk. On medium power, mix all ingredients for 4-5 minutes.
4. In prepared bundt pan, first add the chopped hazelnuts before pouring in the mixed batter.
5. Place pan in the oven for 60 minutes, until golden brown. Inserted toothpick should come out clean.
6. Let stand for 5 minutes to cool.
7. Using a long metal or wooden tip, pierce the bottom 10-15 times before turning cake out onto a serving platter. Once removed from the baking pan, pierce the top of the cake as well to allow for the glaze topping to fully saturate the cake.

Hazelnut Liquor Glaze

Ingredients:

- ∞ 1 stick butter
- ∞ ¼ cup water
- ∞ 1 cup granulated sugar
- ∞ ½ cup hazelnut liquor

Hazelnut Liquor Glaze Directions:

1. In a medium saucepan, combine butter, water, and sugar on medium heat for 5 minutes, stirring constantly.
2. Remove from heat and stir in hazelnut liquor.
3. Lightly drizzle the glaze over the warm Hazelnut Liquor Cake. The pierced cake will continue to absorb the glaze so continue drizzling more across the top, middle, and sides.

Double Chocolate Cricket Crispies

Cooking time: 15 minutes
Yield: 25 servings

Double Chocolate Cricket Crispies

Our team was back in the kitchen prepping for an upcoming party and created these Double Chocolate Cricket Crispies that will be a tasty treat at your next party! This recipe uses about 145+ crickets in the cricket protein powder to add additional protein and nutrition. This new recipe doesn't require an oven, and only takes about 15-minutes to prepare. For this recipe we combined our cricket powder, rice cereal, marshmallows, chocolate chips, and even peanut butter to create the Double Chocolate Cricket Crispies recipe!

Ingredients:

- ∞ 4 tablespoons butter
- ∞ 1 ½ cups chocolate chips
- ∞ 10oz marshmallows
- ∞ 3 tablespoons creamy peanut butter
- ∞ 2 tablespoons Cricket Flours: 100% Pure
- ∞ 7 cups rice cereal

Directions:

1. In a medium sauce pan melt the butter, 1 cup chocolate chips, and marshmallows together until fully melted on medium heat.
2. Add in the peanut butter and cricket powder and stir until fully mixed.
3. Start adding in rice cereal and stir together until the cereal is fully covered by the melted mixture.
4. Using a slightly greased metal pan or glass casserole pan, press the mixture into the container and spread evenly. Pour the remaining ½ cup of chocolate chips across the top of the mixture and lightly press down. Enjoy!

Strawberry Chocolate Ice Cream Shake

Prep time: 10 minutes

Strawberry Chocolate Ice Cream Shake

The humble milkshake is, unfortunately, often overlooked. Yet this easy-to-make dessert packs all the deliciousness your sweet-tooth's dream about. This ice cream shake uses strawberry, chocolate, vanilla ice cream, and cricket flour to craft a dessert that not only tastes delightful, but also provides a great source of nutrition as well. Dive into this guilty pleasure and know that it is a great source of calcium, minerals, nutrients, and protein, as well.

Ingredients:

- ∞ $^1/_3$ cup almond milk
- ∞ ½ cup frozen strawberries
- ∞ 2 tablespoons Cricket Flours: 100% Pure
- ∞ 2 tablespoons chocolate syrup
- ∞ 2 large scoops of vanilla bean ice cream

Directions:

1. In a blender, add frozen strawberries, pure cricket powder, chocolate syrup, and almond milk together.
2. Next, add in 1 scoop of vanilla bean ice cream at a time while blending until smooth.

Cinnamon Baked Apple

Prep time: 7 minutes
Cooking time: 3-4 minutes
Yield: 1

Cinnamon Baked Apple

When apple season rolls around, you have got to try this. You may never eat another raw apple. Don't say I didn't warn you. Our Cinnamon Baked Apple recipe is one that is fast and easy to make. While this recipe uses a microwave, you can also cook these in the oven for a larger number of servings or for a party. These apples taste even better with a dollop of freshly whipped cream on top.

Ingredients:

- ∞ 1 apple
- ∞ 1 ½ teaspoon butter
- ∞ 2 teaspoons Cricket Flours: 100% Pure
- ∞ 2 tablespoons brown sugar
- ∞ ½ teaspoon cinnamon

Directions:

1. Using a knife, core the apple so that the center and seeds are removed. Cut off the bottom of the core, about 1/4 inch, and use the end to plug up the bottom of the apple.
2. Add the butter to the bottom of the cavity created in the cored apple.
3. In a small bowl, mix together the Cricket Flours: 100% Pure, brown sugar, and cinnamon until evenly mixed. Add the cinnamon-sugar mixture to fill the remaining space in the center of the apple.
4. Place the apple in a glass bowl, and cook in the microwave for 3:30-4:00 minutes on high. (Time dependent on apple size and microwave strength)
5. Let cool for 1-2 minutes until safe to serve.

"Lemony Cricket" Pudding Cake

Prep time: 10 minutes
Cooking time: 40 minutes
Servings: 6-9

"Lemony Cricket" Pudding Cake

This vibrant cake will have you exclaiming "Lemony Cricket!" before you can stop yourself. The "Lemony Cricket" Pudding Cake has a fresh lemon taste that bursts through the soft pudding and crisp top. This simple recipe is a light dessert that is perfect to enjoy in the spring or summer. Unlike other cake recipes, the crust will actually rise to the top.

Ingredients:

- ∞ 3 tablespoons flour
- ∞ 2 tablespoons Cricket Flours: 100% Pure
- ∞ 1 cup sugar
- ∞ ¼ cup lemon juice

- ∞ 1 cup milk
- ∞ ¼ teaspoon salt
- ∞ 1 teaspoon grated lemon rind
- ∞ 2 eggs

Directions:

1. Preheat oven to 350°F. Grease an 8x10 baking pan.
2. Sift flour, cricket powder, sugar, and salt into medium mixing bowl.
3. Mix lemon rind, lemon juice, egg yolks, and milk together in a separate bowl and add to the dry ingredients.
4. In small saucepan, bring 2-3 cups of water to a boil as you begin beating the egg whites.
5. Using an electric mixer and a very clean metal bowl, beat egg whites until stiff peaks form.
6. Fold egg whites into batter and pour into prepared baking pan.
7. Take a second larger casserole pan and add boiled water to fill the bottom 1-2 inches high. Carefully set the 8x10 inch pan in the water, and bake in the oven for 40-45 minutes.
8. Once the top is golden brown, remove and let cool for 5 minutes. Add extra lemon rind to the top for taste.

Dark Molasses Ginger Snap Cookies

Prep time: 10 minutes
Cooking time: 12 minutes
Yield: 35 cookies

Dark Molasses Ginger Snap Cookies

A good ginger snap cookie like this will have you swearing off store-bought cookies forever. Soft, moist, and packed with flavor, these ginger snaps show just how easy it is to incorporate cricket flour into your favorite recipes. While your kids and family may love the flavor, the added cricket flour provides a great source of protein and nutrition in addition to the delicious taste of dark molasses. Enjoy!

Ingredients:

∞ 1 $^2/_3$ cups flour
∞ $^1/_3$ cup Cricket Flours: 100% Pure
∞ 1 cup sugar
∞ 1 egg

∞ ¾ cup shortening
∞ 1 teaspoon ginger
∞ 1 teaspoon baking soda
∞ 1 teaspoon cinnamon
∞ ¼ cup dark molasses

Directions:

1. Preheat oven to 350°F. Have one large cookie sheet ready.
2. Using an electric mixer, add in all ingredients at once and stir on medium-low until the shortening is fully mixed in.
3. Use a spoon to portion out each cookie and roll each into a ball before placing it on the cookie sheet, spacing dough 1-2 inches apart.
4. Take a fork and press prongs in the middle of each cookie, first going in one direction, and then next going across those same marks in the other direction, making hash marks.
5. Dust lightly with sugar, and place in oven for 10-12 minutes. Enjoy!

Peanut Butter Chocolate Chip Cookies

Prep time: 10 minutes
Cooking time: 10 minutes
Yield: 24 cookies

Peanut Butter Chocolate Chip Cookies

This new cookie recipe features our Cricket Flours: Chocolate Peanut Butter powder for an added boost of protein, nutrition, and delicious peanut butter flavors. The combination of the semi-sweet chocolate morsels are couple with the smooth rich taste of our cricket protein and peanut butter chips for a tasty treat that is a great afternoon activity for the family!

Ingredients:

- 2 ¼ cups baking flour
- ¼ cup Cricket Flours: Chocolate Peanut Butter
- 1 teaspoon baking soda
- 1 teaspoon salt
- 2 sticks softened butter
- ¾ cup granulated sugar
- ¾ cup brown sugar
- 1 teaspoon almond extract
- 2 eggs
- 1 cup semi-sweet chocolate morsels
- 1 cup peanut butter chips

Directions:

1. Preheat oven to 375°F. Have one large cookie sheet ready.
2. In a mixing bowl add together the baking flour, Cricket Flours: Chocolate Peanut Butter, baking soda, and salt and set aside.
3. In a standard kitchen mixer start to beat on medium power the softened butter, sugars, and almond extract. Mix in both eggs, and set to the mixer to low and slowly start adding the flour mixture to the mixing bowl until fully combined.
4. Remove the mixing bowl from the mixer and fold in the two cups of semi-sweet chocolate morsels and peanut butter chips.
5. Using a standard cookie baking sheet evenly spoon out the cookie dough onto the sheet before placing in the preheated oven for 10 minutes until golden brown.

Weight Conversions

ounces	grams
1	28
2	57
3	85
4	113
5	142
6	170
7	198
8 (1/2 pound)	227
9	255
10	284
11	312
12	340
13	369
14	397
15	425
16 (1 pound)	454
24 (11/2 pounds)	680
32 (2 pounds)	907
35.3 (1 kilogram)	1000
40 (21/2 pounds)	1124
48 (3 pounds)	1361
64 (2 pounds)	1814
80 (5 pounds)	2268

Temperature Conversions

Common Temperature Conversions

ounces	grams
32 (freezing point of water)	0
110	43.3
120 (rare red meat)	48.9
130 (medium-rare red meat)	54.4
140 (medium red meat)	60
145 (extra-moist poultry breast)	62.8
150 (medium-well red meat)	65.6
155 (medium-well standard poultry breast)	68.3
	71.1
160 (well-done meat)	87.8
190 (subsimmering water)	93.3
200 (simmering water)	100
212 (boiling water)	135
275	148.9
300	162.8
325	176.7
350	190.6
375	204.4
400	218.3
425	232.2
450	246.1
475	260
500	273.9
525	287.8
550 (max oven temperature)	

Acknowledgments

Thank you to my parents, Sue and Tom,

for continuing believing in me and always helping to bring my ideas to life. Growing up in such an amazing family is truly a blessing, and working together to share some of our family's favorite recipes brings back cherished memories of late-night baking sessions preparing cinnamon pull-a-parts for the holidays, or making dishes for our weekly family dinners.

to my brother Richard,

for being our FIRST customer and always taking the time to talk over new business ideas and creations. I still remember sitting at your kitchen table that night when I decided it was finally time to launch CricketFlours.com.

to my sister Christine,

for donating your kitchen and your continuous patience for our cricket flour baking experiments!

to my niece Hannah,

for being my taste-tester for each and every recipe featured in this cookbook and those that never made it out of the kitchen.

to my best friends, Bryan, Thomas, Thanh, Dominic, and David,

I think I would need to write a book to thank each of you for everything…and maybe someday I will! Thank you for always being there to brainstorm new product names, flavors, and being willing taste-testers for my newest recipes.

to all of my family members, neighbors and friends,

thank you for the amazing feedback and support for every recipe and dish in this book. Thank you for allowing Cricket Flours to constantly be the topic of our conversations and for always popping up on your news feeds with news and updates. You are truly the best!

Success Stories

Since launching www.CricketFlours.com, we have been working hard to bring new recipes and mixes that you can use in your own kitchens. Our blog and social media follows have created a great community where we love to share what we are working on, and different recipe success stories. Because cricket flour is packed with iron, calcium, B12, protein, and more, it is exciting to see how people are using our different products. The emails we receive on a daily basis continue to inspire use to do more and bring this amazing sustainable and environmentally friendly protein to our audience.

We have collected some of our favorite quotes and messages from our Cricket Flours fans and have included them in this book to highlight our journey and to share their stories. Enjoy!

"It's been on my "To Do" list for quite some time to be able to use cricket flour as part of my daily protein intake, and now I'm lucky enough to do so! There's no denying the sustainability of cricket flour and that means so much to me as a consumer. Better for the environment and delicious? Sign me up!"

- Anne Haugaard

"I've been waiting for something like Cricket Flour for a long time. I love backpacking and this stuff is not only delicious, it is a great source of protein and carbs at light weight. Perfect for powering though a long day on the trail!"

- Alexis John

"As avid foodies, we are completely open to new cooking experiences & recipes. When we heard about Cricket Flours, we were excited to try out an alternative to all-purpose white flour. We knew that Cricket Flour was used for baking purposes, but our inclination was to try it with savory recipes. The day we received our Cricket Flour we prepared a Parmesan chicken recipe for dinner substituting Cricket Flour for regular flour. It was delectable! To top it off, since Cricket Flour provides more protein than regular flour, we felt more full and satisfied with smaller proportions. We could not be more pleased and we look forward to making Cricket Flour a staple ingredient in our home kitchen!"

- Alyssa Windell & Andrew Powell

"Sooooo much yum yum in my tum tum."

- Matthew Gurnick

"Not only do I think Cricket Flours is a great idea, but I have been fortunate enough to try the product already in brownie form. Delicious! Not only are Cricket Flours products tasty and healthy, but good for our environment. It is a win all around! I look forward to supporting their products in the future."

- Jordan Bailey

"It's so nice to be able to include my son in a healthy lifestyle that with a tasty new protein shake that is natural, and safe for us both to enjoy! We love Cricket Flours!"

- MaryPat & Benjamin

"I tried the cricket protein powder the other day at a start up event. I was quite impressed by the taste. However, I am even more excited about the Eco-friendly alternative to existing protein powders.
Keep up the good work!"

- Eric Harvey

"I was skeptical about trying cricket flours at first but understand it is a good source of protein so was willing to give it a try. I've had it in smoothies, milkshakes and baked goods and have found you really can't taste that it's there . . . a good way to get extra protein!"

- Christine & Mike

"Cant wait for my order to arrive! For someone like myself who is extremely particular about his foods ingredients, this Cricket Protein Powder looks like it's going to be a game changer!"

- Bryan Edwards

"I was a little skeptical at first, however, I am glad I tried Cricket Flour. I am an endurance athlete and need high quality protein for before and after my workouts. I was challenged to do the Whole 30 program during January 2015…so I had to find a good alternative to my usual protein shakes. Thank you for a quality product and prompt customer service."

- Jacolyn Wheatley

"The Cinnamon Cricket Flour muffins are some of the best I've ever tasted in my life. I ate my first one 5 minutes into a meeting, at the end of an hour, I had eaten 6."

- Nate Gurol

"I was a little hesitant to try the all cricket protein powder, but I'm glad I did! I mix in a scoop of the powder with my protein shakes and I can't taste a difference. Once I got over the stigma of what I was eating, the nutritional benefits became obvious. I'm glad I decided to give it a try."

- Chris Beattie

About Cricket Flours LLC

Cricket Flours LLC was founded to bring a sustainable and environmentally friendly source of nutrients to our Western cultures. Inspired by global trends, our products and flavors are targeted towards the dietary needs and tastes of our target markets with delicious flavors and product combinations. Our founder first discovered cricket protein when his own dietary allergies forced him to search for alternative food ingredients.

In order to further reduce our company's own carbon footprint, our crickets are sourced directly from farms based in North America and raised for human consumption in FDA registered facilities. To learn more about our company and see our full product line, visit our website at www.CricketFlours.com. To contact our team directly about any questions or finding retail stores near your location, please send us an email at Team@Cricketflours.com or give us a call at 503.383.9218.

Special Coupon Code

As a special thank you for your continued support we included a special 10% OFF coupon code available through this new publication of our Cricket Flour Cookbook: All Cricket, No BULL... Simply go to our main website at www.CricketFlours.com and enter the coupon code **EFGS14D2** on your shopping cart before check out to use the special discount.

Cricket Flours Product Lines

Cricket Flours: 100% Pure

Our Cricket Flours: 100% Pure is our flagship product that is great to use in any recipe. The product is made with only cricket protein that is milled into a fine grain powder. The crickets are sourced directly from farms based in North America to reduce our own carbon footprint to deliver a sustainable and environmentally friendly source of protein and nutrition. Our Cricket Flours: 100% Pure line sells in our 1/4lb, 1/2lb, 1lb, and 25lb packaging.

Cricket Flours: Peruvian Chocolate

Our Cricket Flours: Peruvian Chocolate is a mix of our pure cricket powder and organic Peruvian cocoa powder. This mix is a great option for shakes, smoothies, baked goods, and more with the notes of hazelnut and cocoa. This product was also the signature ingredient in our national launch of the Oreo Mudpie Cricket Milkshake with Wayback Burgers. To see the shake and see a great Buzzfeed video that has reached over 1.8 Million views, visit our website at http://www.cricketflours.com/buzzfeed-cricket-milkshake. Our Cricket Flours: Peruvian Chocolate line sells in our 1/4lb, 1/2lb, and 1lb packaging.

Cricket Flours: Chocolate Peanut Butter

Our Cricket Flours: Chocolate Peanut Butter is made with our pure cricket powder, organic Peruvian cocoa powder, and dehydrated peanut butter. The added peanut butter adds a smooth and creamy texture to your favorite shakes and smoothies. Our Cricket Flours: Chocolate Peanut Butter line sells in our 1/4lb, 1/2lb, and 1lb packaging.

All Purpose Baking Flour

Our All Purpose Baking Flour is made with a blended mix of flours and our pure cricket powder for added protein and nutrition. This mix is crafted to be a one-for-one substitute for any all purpose baking flour so it can be used in your own favorite recipes. Our All Purpose Baking Flour product line sells in our 1lb packaging.

Cricket Fuel Product Lines

Our Cricket Fuel product line comes in our three signature flavors: 100% Pure – Original Flavor, Peruvian Chocolate, and Chocolate Peanut Butter. These packages are designed to provide 10g of protein per packet to take with you on the go, to the gym, or on your next camping trip for added protein and nutrition. Don't see your favorite flavor? Let us know what flavor your want to try next!

Cricket Instant Oatmeal: Cinnamon Raspberry

Our Cricket Instant Oatmeal: Cinnamon Raspberry flavor is the perfect way to start your morning. Just add 1 cup of hot water to this delicious combination of rolled oats, real raspberries and more! This product comes in our in our new kraft packaging in a single serving pouch with 7g of protein per package.

Cricket Brownie Mix: Chocolate

Our newest addition to the Cricket Flours product line is our new Cricket Brownie Mix: Chocolate flavor! We have been working on this new product for the past 6-9 months, but once we got interviewed for Oprah's O Magazine February issue, we knew we had to launch this new gluten free brownie mix. We launched the product first through Kickstarter and raised over $25,000 to launch this new product and can't wait for you to try it! This product makes 20 brownies per package, and contains double the protein compared to brownie mixes typically found on store shelves.

About the Author

Charles B. Wilson is Founder & CEO of CricketFlours.com and the author the Cricket Flour Cookbook, "All Cricket, No BULL…" Charles is based out of Portland, Oregon and first began experimenting crickets after being diagnosed with a list of food allergies. Growing up, Charles' family had been gluten free, but after learning that he would need to remove other ingredients from his diet, crickets became the perfect option to provide a great source of protein and nutrition.

Charles' inspiration to write this cookbook was to craft delicious recipes that feature new ways to use cricket powder in delectable dishes. Often recipes call for special equipment, rare ingredients, etc. Charles wanted to create a cookbook that showcased recipes that could be made with all of the ingredients you already have on hand in your own kitchens.

Charles is often found developing new recipes and products in our facilities, working on new additions to our website, or working with new businesses to collaborate and launch new products and recipes using cricket protein. If you would like to connect with Charles about new recipes or working together, please contact our team at 503.383.9218 or send an email to Charles@CricketFlours.com.

Recipe Notes:

Recipe Notes:

Recipe Notes:

Recipe Notes:

Made in the USA
Coppell, TX
23 November 2019

11840776R00102